Blue Butterfly

A Journal through the Peruvian Jungle

• • •

James Ross Mankoff

Published independently by James Ross Mankoff

For permission requests or to send correspondence
to the author, contact:
James Ross Mankoff
www.jamesmankoff.com

For privacy reasons, some names, numbers, locations,
and dates may have been changed.

First Edition
ISBN 979-8-218-42089-5

· · ·

PREFACE

This journal is a love letter to my
my wife. A love letter to myself.
It is a journey into the depths of
the Amazon Rainforest, a journey
to unblock, to drink sacred
Ayahuasca and to show up in the
world more authentically. It is
about a continued connection to
to nature, to learn, to manifest, to
love and let go.

This is the real, raw, in the
moment: me. An unfiltered
account of my thoughts and
emotions as I navigate my
journey through Peru. To publish
this is in contrast to protecting
my inner child. It is a way of

freeing myself from my mask.
My 'shield'. Sharing this with
you is part of my liberation.

. . .

I've always seen the world
differently. Color, light, energy...
Everything is communication.
Time feels like a conversation,
undulating as I interact with it,
and I perceive my surroundings
with a heightened sense of
understanding. The more I tune in,
the more I feel I am not just an
observer or a participant, but
an active communicator with
the universe.

A recent Neurodivergent diagnosis

upheld the notion that my brain processes information differently than others. I experience the world with greater intensity and feel the need to share these thoughts and emotions of differentness in order to thrive. I believe in honoring my authenticity to emotional experiences. My expressions convey much introspection. My quietness can feel dominant. My words can be forthright and people can have diverse reactions to my presence. When I connect to another – it's magnetic, but when misunderstood, reactions can be defiant or avoidant.

I am athletic, but often trip over nothing. I'm extremely organized, but constantly misplace things.

I laugh out loud at my own thoughts and it can be hard to keep my mind present when it wants to fly away in the clouds.

I love science, math, breaking the rules and creating. I love to be cornered in a box and solve my way out of it. I'll drop a drink in my hand because I forgot it was there.

I'm curious about everything. Like everything. Especially the smallest, most random things. That's usually the best. I have visceral experiences with my passions. I'll hyperfocus, learning all I can absorb and before I know it, I've added another "hobby" to my endless repertoire of specializations.

I've been trying to hide versions of myself to seem "normal" for most of my life, but when I embrace my authentic Neurodivergent self and intuition: magic happens.

· · ·

Three years had passed since the pandemic began; my emotional state was in pieces and I began seeking help. My wedding year brought up deeply rooted trauma from early in our relationship, a shaman abandoned her work to unblock me, my career couldn't find its legs and I began exploring my Neurodivergent diagnosis.

I was lost.

• • •

I had been intimidated by
Ayahuasca since I first learned
of this sacred hallucinogen many
years back, yet I knew at some
point, when the time was right,
I would work with her. Something
in me felt compelled to be open,
that now might be the time to
work with what is often referred
to as the 'mother of all plant
medicine.'

I was listening ...
and then the signals came.

I was 'pulled'; a spiritual dragging to drop everything and start working with her immediately. My wedding was approaching and there was a small window of opportunity. My wife, Moana, was supportive of this journey, but her concerns of exploring the unknown just weeks before our marriage resonated with me.

We did't know how I might show up in the world when I returned.

So I was patient and shortly after our wedding, I began my preparations...

It was time to go to the Amazon.

Peru, 2023

<u>Prep:</u>
Maya - illusion of self
Samadhi - enlightenment.
  to realize the (sameness) oneness
  in all things. Union.
  Everything is one.

imminent self : true nature

- - - - - - - - - - - -

I'm feeling <u>unblocked</u> after
I commited to photo assisting,
after starting my Aya diet,
once I prepaired myself for
this experiance. —it exists and
   - Hotel at Lima. available and on sale.
   - Money back after flight
    change.
   - Money back after paying
    Mindscape final bill.
   - Ojai Apt avail showing date
    change.
   - No rain to Brians when I drove.
   - 10 free film rolls @ Dexters

*I want to ~~return~~ <u>find</u> to my inner child.

*I want to connect with society; to learn to harmonize with it...even if I don't understand or agree with its modern ways. (NO TV, PODCASTS,)
(interference for)
(weeks.)
(while prepaing for)
Maybe taking care of my this)
body → eating healthy... is also helping me unblock.

(~~wonder~~ wonder why we never
(exchange souls, or) "bump" our soul out of our physical bodies. It's attached...until death of the body?

I woke up at the airport feeling scared.

I'm so sad. I don't want to
cause Moana any more pain.
It's hard. My intensions are all
love. I trigger her so hard at
times. I feel so much pain.
I just want to love her. I
want her to heal. I'm
scared to come home to her.
I don't mean to trigger her.
It causes both of us so much
pain. Please Moana, forgive me.
I am not my old self. I worked
and am working so hard to
change. My heart feels ripped from
my soul everytime I see her in
pain. Pain that I cause. Iquitos:

Imeaditly upon exiting the plane
I felt comfort in Iquitos. I
love 3rd world latin countries.
But, it's the land. I feel it.

intensions:
- meet my trueself (inner child)
  (Become)
- unblock my relationship w/ $
- Modern ~~sex~~ Society:
     learn to connect to it.
     harmonize w/ it.

(I have diarrhea.) → Drink coconut
I'm dizzy too.   milk/H₂0

I'm ready to ~~surrender~~ **SURRENDER.**

⬇IDEA⬇
Start a new notebook ... "The time I..."
- watched elk dance on a black
  sand beach
- ... continue this concept of my
  experiances.
- sitting Bulls nephews inipi.
- watched a log internally combust.

Yagua → Tribe I met with NuNv.
           (yah·gwah)

when I arrived in Peru I was 'on guard!'
After spending time in Nicaragua
and Mexico I am used to being
cautious. I'm realizing that the
people here are more gentle. The
street vendors are very aggressive,
but I've learned to talk to some
and Ignor others.

Most of the tourism, nearly all of it,
seems to be related to Ayahuasca.
The vendors sell neon paintings from
their own experiance with the plant
along with necklaces lined with
Ayahuasca seeds. →Mick

One of the vendors offered me a
private boat ride tour of the river
yesterday, but I could not find him
today. So I sat down, ate my
breakfast and waited for the day
to present itself.

I watched a large vendor selling
necklaces to a tourist. He had a
calm energy and I thought → how
nice it would be if he had a boat.

his name was <u>NuNu</u> and he had the largest Jaguar claw around his neck. He had a boat! and agreed to take me out on the Amazon River today. He works just enough to make money and go back into the deep jungle where he is from. ~~money~~ Many of the street vendors are this way. His father is a Master plant medicine Shaman. NuNu is sweet and I felt comfortable on a private tour with him. He was so excited to get this work → That felt
. . . .   good.

<u>Terry</u> - N. Carolina/Greece boy doing a 6 month Dietas. +1 555 666 0715 we had 2 lovely meals together.
Aya saved his life.

• visited Monkey Island. saw dolphins. Met a Yagua tribe. Felt like a tourist... All day.   yagua = yahua

• when visiting the <u>yagua tribe</u>, I felt a push & pull of them wanting my money and myself, the tourist, exploiting them. I just wanted to meet them, but I suppose knowing that option is available is already part of the problem.

<u>I manifested my entire day today</u>

The Yagua performed for me. They pandered me. I assume most tourists want to blow a blow gun or dance w/ a tribe, but it just felt uncomfortable to me. I was also,... ~~all~~ all by myself → which was pleasant. Many mixed emotions.

I should learn to relax on the way to my destinations.

Iquitos is so empty! My thoughts are slowing down. I can take my time writing them.

I briefly spoke to a man who came back from 2 weeks at my retreat. I could feel himself lighter & happier. He was missing a leg. I wonder if he was a soldier.

Life feels like I'm in a dream. Everything is a little psychedelic. Some of the visuals... are just so strong...They VIBRATE.

It feels good to slow down

My body feels strange here. Maybe its the diet. or the dehydration. Ayahuasca calling. OR a constant hunger? I feel buzzed.

I am ready

I'm excited

MINDSCAPE
↓
My retreat for 2 weeks.

Live in "the now". Live in the present moment. STOP thinking about the future.

I am nervous. I am scared. I AM

Everyone seems so happy here. All the people in the streets. They are all happy. All the couples holding each other. Children playing. It's all happy here.

There is no ~~need~~ ~~to have~~ both ~~red~~ traffic and pedestrian lights when just a traffic light will do.

It's ~~strange~~ difficult having someone like Taylor in my life when I cannot just let them out of my life. I think Norman was the only other relationship I've had where I felt I needed to be a false version of me in order to "keep the peace" and navigate the complexities of keeping that relationship going while being hurt by them in the process.

Moana suggests that I stand up for myself now and I'm trying to understand how to do ~~that~~ amicably. Normally I would just walk away (and tell them why)... but that doesn't feel like an option. I want to confront Taylor in the moment, but it can be hard when triggered.

There was a white ameican "Burning Man" dress "cowboy" playing American songs loud in the street. He was making a fool of himself, but really → he showed me not to care so much about what others think of me.

I want to wear my NEW necklaces. I shouldn't care how I am perceived. I usually don't, except I'm in a foriegn place and I'm usually "on guard" until the place doesn't feel foriegn anymore.

ooooo

Let go of what has passed
Let go of what may come
Let go of what is happening now
Don't try to figure anything out
Don't try to make anything happen
Relax, right now
and rest
    - Tibetan teaching

The clouds here are spectacular

watching the "cowboy" clean up his "performance" space (TRASH) during his morning excersize routine was beautiful. Than his prayer that followed was a bit crazy

I've enjoyed watching the boats gently
navigate the river, which
millions of years ago
once
flowed in the opposite direction ←→

○○○

It will be a full moon tonight. Tonight
is my 1st ceremony. When I am in flow
these special happenings/occurances are
normal experiances. This happens all the time

●●●

The city became more gentle as soon as
I settled into it.

○○○

I am aware that these special occurances
that happen to me regularly is rare.
I am special. ← when I feel this, I am powerful
Moana has pointed out that this feeling
can also come with ego. Feeling
"Better than" others. Yet this is not how
I feel, but I do care to make sure I
am not projecting this.

WOAH

I

AM

50

sensitive

Tapping w/ Lucia. meeting my innerchild.
Neon colors, Flushing diarrhea. Next round,
vibrating body. Penetrating everywhere. smell.
Body Pain. Hello, nice to meet you.
Alien. Kubrick meets star wars. chanting.
less then 8 people. chads missunderstang,
caring energy. I've had to protect myself for
so long. I need a safe space to be me.
Reptil, snake... → Plant! Too intense for
me. Full on trippy Balls. Lucias voice.
waiting to start. smallest dose. I can't
stop my diarrhea. Electric. Vibrational.
Mother. Wamb. Probing specific parts of
me. So agressive at first. Attacking.
Slow. It's own slow rythem → non stop.
Rainbow of colors. Eyes closed for the
first Half. ~~The hardest half.~~ Chad looked
Pixelaited. Pixels. Hard to stand. Help to
the bathroom. Safe space. I understand.
I cannot beleive people dedicate their
lives to this. I felt an equal understanding
of my experience to the shamans. I got it.
I'm so pure. I'm so connected. I'm so
sensative. I don't Know how to be me
in society because I'm soooo sensative.
Moana sees my inner child. My parents tried
to protect me. Female. I'm infinitly more
Sensative then those around me. Dietas
tastes like garlic. Beautiful space.

I cannot even imagine the souls of other plants. The possibities to explore are endless. I don't know if I want too. She morphs. twists. contorts. Has a heartbeat that is still, yet moving. She's old, wise. Can probably cure many things. She is not for everyone. I'm intimadated. speechless. words cannot describe meeting her. Everyone In the room experienced her together. It was not a seperate experiance, but ~~diffent~~ people will interpret it all differently. "Name the color, blind the eye". Maybe just a drop on my tounge is enough... maybe just a smell. I'm not sure I enjoyed the experiance. one girl puked super early on. I thought I'd never trip. It took a long time to kick in. I almost gave up waiting. Lucia and I sang together. She ~~said~~ followed my lead. It was magic. There was Ramon too. another shaman. another singer. This is hard work. It felt very similar to my ACID overdose. ← That helped me through this. It's nothing like any other psychodelic. It's an experience of her. She was the master. [END]

I need rest. I am a bright light. [Following morning]
I was Killed. How do I show it and
...kinda. feel safe?

Chad was so calm.
        Then came the 'Relaxed Period'.
I am so sensative, but that should not be
percieved as a weakness.

I cannot believe there are so many
plants shamans work with. I do not
want to be this type of shaman...
I think.
I lost a lot of nutrients through
my purge.
Lucias face while singing to me
moved and change with her voice.
it was so surreal. so Alien.
is it possable she removed my Anxiety?
will society bring it back?
Did Lucia heal me too?
Lucias voice → MY GOD.

Being around Taylor is the least safe
space in my world right now.
Maybe in a very very long time.
Taylor's super unhealthy for me.

was my brain | I need to be
getting reprogramed? | protected

Hello, nice to meet you.

After nearly giving up on meeting her, I laid down once more and I started to feel a buzz through my body. A massaging ▮ body rub through my pores. For a long time it was pleasant, I thought for sure based on the size of my cocktail that this would be all of my experience. A nice body buzz with no visuals. So I decided to close my eyes. ~~she~~

Slowly, I could make out some colors. Faint at first. Opening my eyes would make them go away. Keeping them closed, I started to see my first patterns.

The next stage happened rather quickly. Aggresively. A blinking, neon, electric organism that moved like a snake started to penitrate me from all directions at once. Like a hug, but with intension of where it probed,

or caressed it self on top of me.
Its movement was in multiple dimensions.
its rythem and pace was like a scene
in a sci-fi movie where the whole
screen gets filled with a giant
mothership slowly moving through
the frame. ~~Some times~~

Her tenticles, like an Octapus,
attacked me so fiercely ⇒ I can
see why people fight back. Piercing
my Brain, my arms, my stomach,...
She seemed to know exacty where she
was going.

I was not affraid, but it was so
painful that I wanted it to end.
A boa constrictor times 20 wrapping
herself all over me. Slithering.
I suppose in retrospect I was being
killed, but it didn't feel that way
in the moment.

She ~~wanted to~~ completely consumed me until I became part of her. She was always in control.

I would remember from my mushroom trips ~~that~~ movement helped, so I would sit up or try to jiggle my hands or body to try to ease the experiance. It helped momentarily, but was useless. I gave up, I was a long for the ride. I couldn't wait for it to stop.

yet, something told me she was healing me. pinpointing areas in me that needed to be healed / removed. She worked on me like a body worker, a massage theripist...

It lasted quite a long time. the attacking part that is. And then, and I don't remember the exact transittion, but she eased off the attack and Presented herself to me. I was now meeting Ayahuasca.

she floated.   Looking down on me
she spread her wings. metephoricly
speaking → well, I suppose this is all
a metephor ... Staring at me without
eyes she began to present her
show. A showing that would last
the rest of the night.

Her movements still resembling a
ship moving through water... She
passed right to left. She was no
longer agressive, but my body and
stomach were sick and uncomfortable.
It was difficult to sit back and
enjoy.

Her colors were only electric neon
colors. A full rainbow spectrum
that resembled an advanced black
light painting. It wasn't for me... the
colors were not my taste.

I remember thinking I did not need
the necklace NuNu gave me for
protection. The sharp claw of
a Jaguar strung around my neck

lost its value a little to me. Relying on it only seemed like a symbol. And f the Ayahoscar Ayahusca branch adorned next to it is an off putting color. It doesn't feel bright enough for me.

She moved left to right, but off Kiltered. A perfect harmonic movement. She took visual breaks but not for long and the breaks were intermissions for the next show.

She moved up and up and up. She was Symetrical and Architectual. like a ship. a space ship. Architectual.

until she was not.

She showed me, only a couple of times, her womb. It was a voulnerable place, even for her. It felt like her heart, and also that of a pregnant baby belly. It was the hardest visual to interpert. It was kind of a cylander with and oval womb. It was more complex then I could understand. It was the most organic part of the experiance.

The shamans singing finally made sense. Like playing the flute to a Cobra. It hypnotized it. The songs were a prayer to her. A worship. They connected and elevated the experiance.

Ramon's voice was nice, but Lucias voice was a gift. They took turns chanting and smoking Mapacho, a Jungle tobacco. I smoked it to but I don't care for it. It was used in Ritual on our bodys along with Paulo Santo incense. My favorite incense. Lucias voice vibrated. shifted. morphed. it was alien and calming. Its rythm unlike any song I've heard before. I couldn't appreciate it until I met Ayahuasca.

Lucia and I shared a moment. One of the most special of my trip. I was feeling very connected, pure, in tune. She had been singing for a while. I laid on my stomach, over the foam matress on the floor. I was coming down from my "trip" and feeling

better. I felt so connected to her song
I started tapping on the wood floor.
Gently, but in rythem with her.
The drum sound I made amplifed
the song and I continued a consistent
beat with her for quite some time.

I was aware how sacrid these songs
were and singing with her seemed
like a big "NO NO". But my intuitions
told me to keep tapping... Then the
moment came when it was time to
finish. I slowed my tapping and her
voice followed. As I slowed, I changed
my rythem and her voice followed.
until I slowly... ended... with a
soft brush of my finger on the
floor.

Magic.

I laughed. I tapped the floor a bunch.
I was out of rythem and I wasn't
trying to be. I knew I may have
been too aggressive now with my

tapping in this moment and I
agreed with Chad when he asked
me to stop.
(I should talkabout Chad later.)

Then the purge came. Endless diarriah.
That scared me the most. I want to
maintain a healthy body in the Jungle.

Time passed and I had come down
quite abit. The last stage was visual
with my eyes open. Everything was part
of a pixelated Matrix. It was fun to
look at. My body still felt very sick.

Ramon and Lucia took turns with
each of us. Chanting directy to the
individual. Finishing with long breaths,
blowing over their bodies. I knew
when it was my turn. I would face
Lucia.

When I sat down in front of her
she was backlit by the full moon
lighting the jungle. I could see her body
but not her face. I was right in front
of her.

She started her song. moving her face in all directions. projecting her vabrato all over. I felt pretty sober up until this point. until I saw her face.

It vibrated in the dark. It was not still. It left a trail behind its movements. A 5 second shutter drag that gave her many eyes and mouths that desolved and appeared in front of me. She felt so Alien. She was special.

I asked her to heal my diarrhea. I cryed inside for my body to make it through this safley. My mind and soul were fine. The ask was silent, but communicated.

She finished her song and placed her hands on my head. She took deep Breaths and blew on my head while finding pressure points. Then she went to my hands to finish.

- I can understand how Terrys 1st time he asked for 'unconditional love'. I can see how this plant provides that to people. For me though, It was so painful on my body. Its not really a loving feeling... but without that pain. It could be.
- I'm the only one here taking seclusion and silence (others on the dietas are also doing) (no touching).
- It's almost noon and I'm feeling better.
- Ayahuasca started working with me as soon as I heard her calling. She doesn't tell me what to do. She opens me up to look inside myself. I think. I'll explore her more.
- Talk more on the jungle / Mindscape.
- We compair her to animals (reptiles, but she is so different than that. Movies have actually done an ok job of prepairing the visual when you put together many diffent shows.
- Aya is not a god. She is just one of the many powers in our vast world. But unlike many → she lets us experiance her.
- I do not want Taylor in my life any more. Maybe I just need to tell Taylor.
- These reflections sound more beautiful then the pain of the experiance itself.

Meeting my inner child

I am a bright, beautiful, loving, kind
creative + exceptually sensative
being. I feel so much. These sensativites
let me "tune in". → To soo much.
To everything living and what we as
humans typically perceive as "not
alive". I'm playful. I like to play with
everything I'm sensative too. my
play is humorous, creative, intelectual,
~~sensative~~... and what I play with,
plays back to me.
I'm so loving and free. So femanine.
I frolick. I'm expressive and gentle.
I am delicate
I'm so pure. It's complicated for me
to use ~~verbal~~ language to communicate
my ~~thoughts~~ to most humans. Animals
and plants and the universe might
be easier for me.
It wasn't a complicated or complex meeting.
im so proud of who I am.

My question now is how do I safetly
bring him into our world? ~~it it~~
~~it it~~ the people and society

I ~~surround~~ myself with ↑Feel DO NOT safe.

I believe I need to be _protected_ in order to show up authentically.

This is my next question:

> How do I show up authentically and protect my light in society?

maybe I'm like Prince. In the way he is so special he doesn't really understand how to "be" in society. Unfortunetly he treats society very crevly. A side effect of his gift.

＝＝o＝＝＝o＝＝＝ooooo＝＝＝o＝＝＝o＝＝

meeting my inner child was not a vision. I was my inner child when on Aya. I experienced it first hand.

＝＝o＝＝＝o＝＝＝oooooo＝＝＝o＝＝＝o＝＝

Funny how my Aya bed is next to Chads. Both my Aya bed and my sleeping bed have a light smell of some elses body order. This place is clean, but this is jungle living. All the yoga matts smell like feet too. The sheets have stains. I smell. But It feels like real living. I am enjoying it.

Eating GMO is eating souless food.
Alestor Crowley — Tarot Cards.
Mindscape is protected. A shamen came to bless the property many years ago.

most are open to me being silent and "appearing" to be not engaging. on the contrary. I'm just opening up and here to listen and engage in a different way. One man confronted me about it. It offended him that I wasn't "participating". It was painful to hear his sorrow projected onto me. I just listened and projected love to him. He didn't understand.
compassion ____ . ____

I watched all the Ayahuaska poured. When it was my turn I was poured the smallest portion of all. Less then a half, where a half to full was the norm, I'm so sensative it rocked me so hard. Next time I think the correct amount is a drop. Just enough to seep into my body...no more...I may even just smell it. I think it's that powerful with me.
I now understand Andrews pain. He couldn't go further. I get it. He resisted the purge. I am going to keep going.

Edward asked me if I would nod to yes/no questions. He loved my ~~si~~ silence. He asked if I would be his creative coach. I shared my journal w/ him. He's done Aya 17 times and said he always wanted my experiance. Inspiring him feels good. He returned calming advice about my next session and encouraged me to not back off the dose too much. I think I'll try half of what I did.

LET GO

Yoga here is nice. This is a wellness Retreat.

This place is the real deal. A true healing center.

Everyone here is strong. They all enjoy a challenge... like me.

Chad is my challenger. my Taylor... but easier.

I closed my eyes and Ramon spent time sucking and spitting out (energy?) from me. His ritual was supposed to help. I didn't feel anything.

Ramon did a private healing on me. He said I was very sad. He said I brought a book with me but I won't be ready to read it until the end of the retreat. He is right. He also said he's going to give me my 5th sense back. Book: Rick Rubin, The Creative act.

I woke up to a disheveled room with stuffing (cotton) all over the floor and my belongings piled in the center of the room. It rained last night. Down poured. The first since I've been in Peru.

Earlier in the evening I drank my second Ajo Sacha Dietas A neon green colored drink liquid that tastes like a light garlic. It's a begginers Dietas. As I understand it, Dietas are a connection to a plant... in my case → Ajo Sacha... which is traditionaly used by shamans to align themselfs with that plant. Some can spend up too two years alone in the jungle with a single plant. Dietas are the way to become a shaman. To have powers.
• • •

I lied in bed restless from the heat. waiting for the later part of the evening to cool down.

Closing my eyes I started to dream. Dashing small visions speed their way through my mind. Like a picture flip book, a quick time lapse visual presented many visions to me.

I opened my eyes and realized I'm not dreaming. ~~☐~~ the visuals were only when I closed my eyes. I wanted to sleep... to get rest for the following days Aya ceremony, but every time I closed my eyes... More dreams appeared. I was so confused at first.

I was awake, but dreaming. I was Lucid. I kept my eyes closed and watched the show. At times little "friends" appeared. Like bunnies. They were so cute. They were little guides... I kept tossing and turning. I wanted to sleep but these ~~visions~~ Dreams were keeping me awake.

I asked for the rain to come. To cool down the Tambo I am sleeping in. Constantly getting up to urinate, it would break up the "visions" that felt like little visits that constantly shifted. So much to see.

Then the rain came. It poured. The thunder seemed to stay. A constant boom that never subsided. After a few flashes of lightening

I noticed I was also sensitive to my vision experiance. A booming sky glowed from lighting and blinded me. I was so sensitive. I started seeing shaddows around my Tambo, the small hut I slept in. Fear crawled in and I was scared. I closed my eyes, but the dreams were there. They morphed into gentle nightmares. ~~Monsters~~ A friends face turned into a blue monster. Instead of running from this fear. I tried to project love.

I opened my eyes again. My pillow was so uncomfortable. I ripped out half of the cotton stuffing and tossed it on the floor. The fears persisted and I continued to experiance a very light lucid experiance. I couldn't shake it, so I embraced it. And it scared me. The darkness of the

Jungle scared me and I realized I needed the comfort of the people here. Tomorrow I would start talking again. This was a ~~very~~ hard night.

I know that these fears are here to teach me. As soon as I can let go... I won't be scared anymore.

Breathwork

40 mins. Quick breaths. My first time doing breathwork. They said it would be challenging, but I enjoyed it. 40 straight min on my back of heavy breath. Some of the others cryed. I envied that. I want to let go. At times I would slow my breath and I noticed my fingers tingle. My toes, feet vibrated. As I continued, my body vibrated. With 10 deep finishing breaths the practice was almost complete. With my last breath, I drew air in as deep as I could and held it there. It was pleasant so I continued to hold it. I found zen in this moment and I did not want to breath

again. Time passed, every pore in my body tingling with oxygen... I finally released.

And then...

I LET GO.

Zen.

It was my first time in my life experiencing PEACE.

No thoughts. complete and utter peace. I was happy. I cried.

I laid in this state for sometime with my eyes closed. Feeling it.

and then I saw <u>Buddah</u>... gently appearing before me. I've never felt such bliss... A moment of enlightenment? What. A. shift.

This stayed with me for the next hour. I walked so calmly. People said they saw a huge shift. It was such a warm feeling.

I am ready to meet mother Ayahuaska again.

The ceremonies take place in a
Large Tambo, with roughly 12-14
~~beds~~ matresses laid on the floor
along the wall in a circle. It's
nighttime and everyone is quiet while
Palo Santo is moved throughout the
space. After some time, the shamans
start to whistle, welcoming in the
great plants. It's not a loud whistle,
the only noise is the air moving
through ~~their~~ their lips.
And eventually after a long long silence,
Ayahuasca is poured into large two
ounce shot glasses. Each is given a
half glass their first time and then
offered a second round halfway
through the 5-6 hour ceremony.
Those that drank her before,
Two nights before, can choose how
much they want to drink. Some
choose a full glass.

A little bit of time passes and then
the chanting "Ikaros" starts. These shamans are
masters of breath. Singing the entire
time ... but the way in which
they play their instrument, their song

I can not believe how much music comes out in a single breath, on repeat, for hours.

Everyone sees Ayahuasca differntly. My vision will be different from anothers.

Then she cleans you. This is the "purge". For some, its puking...in the bucket next to your bed. For others, yawning, farting, or In my and other peoples case here → shitting.

The bathrooms are close by and an employee or two is here to help You get to and from your mattress... always without touching you.

It's hard dedicated work by the people here who look out for us during our "trip". They do an excellent job keeping us safe while also letting us be. ————————.————————.————————

There is a constant struggle here for me. It's alotof work. Each time you need to get up to go to the bathroom. To drink lots of water. To keep your body

healthy. It's all a little bit masochistic.
I believe many people here have
experienced enough pain in their life
to have developed some tollerence to pain.
But if you've gone through life
sheltered from pain... have you really
opened yourself up to experience it?
Pain is not a bad thing. You can learn
a lot from it. It is a great teacher.

---

listening to everyone's experiences in the
sharing circle was profound. Ayahuasca
provides an oppourtiny to experience
self reflection. When you read about
or are explained a concept → it makes
sense, but understanding through an
epiphany changes your core.

One person said "If my family heard about
this experience they would think I'm
a drug addict"... and we all laughed.
This experience is definitely not that.
It's such hard work with the hopes of
finding "something" which is different
for everyone. everyone is working very hard to
better themselves here.
Nils
~~One man~~ experienced a jaguar coming
in and out of his body. Then sitting

next to him and he realized a
very profound thing about him...
Something that was always there.
To be honest, I can only remember
how emotionally grateful he was for it.
but not what it was.

Another experianced so much pain
that she realized she hates herself.
That she doesn't love herself and she
needs to change that. A realization
that Ayahuaska showed her. She's
scared to do it again. There are
others who have decided not to take
more too, but are enjoying other parts
of the healing process.

I love you Moana. Part of this Journal is to
share with you. For you to understand.

Jungle Tobbacco! When I arrived I really
wanted to take the Dietas seriously. I
learned so much from times in nature
where I don't speak. But they don't follow
those rules here. Its relaxed. I think Its
why I started talking. I felt a little out
of place being the serious one, Maybe
I can take things to serious. Just who I
am.
I am soo hungry: The diet here has been
I want a burger: the same as the prep.

Diet: rice, beans, lettuce, tomato, noodle, potato,
veggie soup. brocolli. carrots. lentals.
watermelon. apple. pear. No salt. Egg.
No oils. Thats it. I wanted a bannana, but
its "too sweet" for my Ajo Sacha Dietas.
often I'm not hungry. It is work to
make me eat. the food is not great.

I have a hemorrhoid from all the "flushing"
They are gonna make me something "purging".
from the Jungle for it. :) CHAD:

Chad offered us to pick our ceremony
beds. The first pick of mine was
his. ha! so I had to pick again and I
choose next to him. It was away from the
door and I liked that Zone. Funny
how I was choosing to be close to one
of my challenges here: Chad.

Like Taylor, he answers →He is as wise as
questions he doesn't | me. There is struggle
fully understand as if | for him there. He
they are truths. | ~~talks~~ talks to
He just bought the place |others with a
3 months ago. He acts |more gentleness
wise but he is not. It |but his under —
is a hard dynamic with |tone is still
us. He knows more about |condisending.
Aya, but I don't feel ⌐

I'm not alone with these thoughts
others struggle with him too.
Both Taylor and him "project" wisdom.
I have a hard time listening to every
word that comes out of their mouth
when they speak to me. He talks to
me differently. It hasn't gone unnoticed
by others. Taylor is much worse for me

Both feel as if they are pretending to
help me because they "should" they have
some responsibility too. But they don't
want too.

I Don't care as much
for Chads wife either.
its hard having both
as authority figures in
the spiritual realm.
They lead discussions
and offer ... "lecture!..,
their opinions as if
they have earned
that authority by
owning this place.
They def are a buzz
Kill. They talk like
they are trained psychologists

Chad was a drug
dealer before he
bought this place.
To their credit thay
it is a well run,
safe space and they
do really care.
unlike Taylor → who
is selfish. Chad
wants to give back.
Thats all he does
by running Mind
scape. He really isn't
That bad. I'm
I'm safe. here OK

There are two puppies + two kittens to play with | We don't eat dinner the day of ceremony.

I think I was really annoyed when the shaman Ramon was doing my private healing and Chad and his wife Allison were my language interpreters but would place their own opinions into the experience. Into his translation.

OK → I'm done venting. No more of that.

When I was offered Ayahuasca a second time I decided to go with 1/4 pour. Thats half the amount of my 1st time. There was a solid body high with gentle no visuals. The body felt similar to the first attack, but much less subdued. Tolerable. After a while I decided I wanted to take another 1/4 dose... why not? I'm already commited. But there were 3 signs that told me not too. I asked Chad for it and he almost poured it, but told me to wait for the second round offering. I knew if I waited I'd have to go for a stronger dose and would have rather

just topped this moment off now w/
¼. Then, my mate next to me went too
deep and Chad spent an hour working
on him. Since Chad won't touch you
during ceremony...he used other methods
to get this guys face out of his puke
bucket. Blowing Machu (tabbacco) smoke
in his face. over and over. Eventully
spitting a water with a protective
medicine (will get name later) energy
at him. It was a huge buzz kill. The
third was when he came after this guy
came back from the bathroom and spilled
his puke bucket onto my side and
onto my Aya glass. The glass that I
would drink from for second helpings.
That was enough signs for me. So
Instead I tried my best to relax and
watch. A lot of puking and such an
impressive display of care from the
staff. They changed puke buckets
regulary and theyput great care into
keeping the space safe emotionaly

for everyone there. I realize this probably sounds a little gross, but its part of the medicines purging process.

I was ~~get~~ greatful that my experience was gentle on me after the last one. The guy next me was ok. He had a profound experience where he entered a state of nothingness. It showed him that nothing mattered. His past didn't matter. The bullshit that surrounds him didn't matter. for him, it seemed. it was a lesson he needed... He wants to take a little less next time. He's curious if he can tame his loss of control.

I don't know if I want another ceremony. I may just ~~continue~~ continue w/th breathwork, yoga, the clean atmosphere to be alone and ponder for the following week. There is another part of me that wants a more profound experience... an epiphany... I still havn't decided.

Did the Ajo Sacha ▮▮▮ I don't know if I
enhance my Breath ▮▮▮ want to suffer
work experience? ▮▮▮ any more.

I know this place is giving me time I need to
reflect. There will be great benefit to that.
Chad suggested that my vision wasn't meeting
Ayahuasca, but meeting my Authentic self.
That, Aya doesn't show herself. I dunno.

• I like the new guy named Carthy ▯ Jungle ▯
  He has never been in a forest! ▯ walks ▯
• lighters do not make good flash lights.
• They say the first ceremony is often
  the hardest. the   2nd is often easier.

During the first   Its not buggy here.
Ceremony I   There is no wind
remember think-   I'm bare foot.
ing.→ To protect   I wear the same
myself. I need to   shirt ✚ shorts.
live isolated enough
surrounded by friends
that could protect me from the   It rained all
outside world. My own little   night again.
Oasis where I could frolic   I had a euphoric
and play.   I am not scared   experience with
                                    Ajo Sacha. A Bliss—
: A teacher : Any more   Full body high. A
: Should be open: ＊＊   Strong powerful one
: to learn from: I can only imagine
: their students.   continuing this
                                    dietas... It would
chad? Taylor?   be a wild plant to
                         have a human connection.

Chad/Taylor talk down to me. They want the last word. I don't know how to react to that, and be my authentic self. My authentic self would stand up and not let them talk to me this way. But instead I stay quiet and repress my emotions. It's unhealthy. I guess I feel standing up for myself will cause even more reaction from them. They won't back down. They will talk down even harder and I cannot just walk away because they are involved in a part of my life that I am fearful to bring stress into... but I suppose... its already there.

Maybe I should start pushing back and standing up for myself. Its not going to be easy to do. I can't always think cleary in the moment when they trigger me. I'm paralyzed. But I have stood up for myself in these situations before. "I hear you, but Maybe I say: "I don't agree... with that" and when they push their point...
"I don't feel comfortable w/ you talking down to me".

I dunno → Brandie will have to help me.
with the wording. I'll have to practice
it. So I'm not too reactionary.
I never would have guessed how toxic both
Taylor and Chad are

I never would have thought that they
would have been one of the things I'd
need to work through here.

> I'm sensitive and need to
> be protected

This is what I learned from my first
drinking ceremony w/ Ayahuasca.
Maybe Moana can help. Maybe I don't
need to face this alone?
Taylor doesn't want to learn from me.
Taylor just wants to lecture. Taylor never
listens. ~~# Taylor~~

Relationships should be mutual.

♡ I LOVE you moana. ♡
  you are my life partner.

I cannot wait to come home to you.

In Brazil, its common to do ▮ ceremony in the light. Peru → in the dark.
I think Colombia they might dance?

It isn't easy to live in the jungle. Luxuries are different here. Small things can provide such nurishment. This feels like real living. Indigenous living.

overflowing bowls of freshly rolled Mapachu.

I'm always the very last to sit down for every meal.

Books are scattered everywhere. Many of them with pages worn down from hundreds of different readers. Lots of medicne books. Aya books, self help books. Even Alice and Wonderland.

I got really worked up over my issues with christianity today. This is something I must LET GO

Sam says Aya is supposed to make you uncomfortable so you can learn. That it will heal and unblock

Ramon gave me his jungle plant medicne for my bum.

He was sick for 2 years and it healed him. It cured Chad of his anxiety on his 1st ceremony.

BOOK : PLANT SPIRIT SHAMANISM. by
Ross Heaven & Howard Charing → about Dietes

I dreamed of being lifted to an elite celebrity status, I didn't care for, while having to navigate bullies and

Moana falling for another person...
it was a hard dream. She still loved
me though. It was very vivid.

I didn't sleep at all last night, I'm going
to be exhausted for ceremony [Lee Holden.]

Each time we do ceremony, we go 18 hours
of fasting between meals.

I did a Chi Gong Class and loved it.
Moana has got to try it. ←

The heat can be pretty unbearable at the
peak of the day. The property is
surrounded by a large pond of lilly pads
whos flowers bloosin in the evenings. Each
day at the hotest hours we go for a swim.
There are 6 small individual Tambos and
one large shared Tambo with bunk
beds. The main Center, which house the
Kitchen and Chads living space   surround
the pond... as well as the large
Ceremony Tambo. The "Maloka" buildings are
made of wood, leaves, and screens that
go floor to ceiling. There is no privacy
but there also is. I mean → we shit
and puke together... So we are family.
There is a hammock in front of my Tambo
that I enjoy writing in. I carry this Journal
and water bottle w/ me everywhere and

switch between wearing the two
necklaces I got from the yagu tribe.
There is a toilet in my Tambo similar
to an outhouse. After I use it, I put
wood chips over my fluids. They haven't
changed it yet. It's been a week.
Laundry is hung along the walkways
and you can occasionally hear neighbors.
It's the Jungle, but it's lived in.

The people who work here are amazing.
Sam - is 6 weeks new to the facility but
he is wise and very in touch with
his new plant Journey here. He is the
one I ask questions too. He's very young.
Ise - leads yoga and has brought me
the feminine kindness and support I need
here. Two
The three of them also help out in
ceremony. What kind people to help
change our puke bowls and guide us
to the bathroom. No one interfers w/
the your ceremony experiance. That
is for you and you alone. Sam says
that Aya is about working in the dark.
A lot of people want to feel good. Aya
is not that medicine. It shows you

your deepest pains. Ones you've
avoided and forces you to address
them. Sam is wise for his age.

There are 9 total guests. 3 about
70 years old. Two of them is their
first plant ~~medicine~~ experiance.
medicine
3 30 year old girls from England. One
has done it a bunch, the others for
their first time. Both the new girls
struggled with a ton of pain the
first two ceremonies and wonder if
they will take Aya for their final
one tonight. The other 3 guys are
close to my age. One with lots of
Aya experiance and the other two
for the first time.

I'm exhausted but I've decided I'll
drink tonight. The same amount as
the first night. This is the work
I came here for. Shortly before the
ceremony I was speaking too some of the
guys about Chad and it was clear he triggers
them too. One said hes almost left 3 times
~~because~~ because of Chad. We started getting
worked up over our frustration with him
and I couldn't ~~shake~~ shake it. I was so ANGRY

I almost didn't ~~drink~~ drink that night.
It reminded me of the anger I held
with Kyle moments before my wedding.
I found a way to drop the ~~emotion~~ in that
moment w/ Kyle. I would not let that
emotion come between Ayahuaska and
me... So I thought of Moana. And my
heart melted. She could move me ~~through~~
this trigger. This would teach me not to let
triggers linger.
Earlier that day, I had decided this
would be my last ceremony and
next week → only the plant dieta...
but really.
                   who knows.

woah.

~~puki~~ puking. Diarrhea. so much pain. what a relief she's going easy. bored. praying mantus. Let's just get right into it shall we:

I was slightly aggrivated by Chad still, but overall, I was able to shake it. when Aya came, she came gently this time. At first, It was a light temple massage. Then she slowly made her way through my body. It was an uncomfortable feeling. Pressure appling in and outside your body. It makes no sense. There is no reference for it. But there she was. And she stayed in this state for quite some time. After a while, I just got bored and asked her to give me some visuals... to entertain me, but she didn't.

I wondered when my purge would start. It had been a while and eventually I went to the bathroom for a light "purge". when I got back, I was over it. This is uncomfortable and pointless. I started to ignor it and tried to sleep... Then a praying mantis appeared before me. Larger then me... it took a huge bite into my being. And in that instant... Pain. Terrible aweful, pain.

where the fuck did she come from and what the fuck is up with this change of pace? I tried to fight it, but I decided it was best to give in.

I heard Lucias voice. she was directing

this attack of pain at me. Each fluxuation
in her tone felt like a knife twist all
over my body.
        OK. OK. ▓▓ ▓▓▓▓.
        I'm listening.
And then, in a explosion of thought
I realize:

One of my necklaces has a bad
spirit in it!

                    • • •
And I ▓▓▓ knew, had always known, it was in
the Jaguar claw.
I had a funny feeling about it after I bought
it, but it took a little while to sink in.
I stopped wearing it when I arrived... It was
just... off putting. Then I realized I don't
want it anymore and my instincts told me
to get rid of it. I didn't know it was bad
yet, or in retrospect, I did but wasn't used
to recognizing this sensation. I debated
giving it to people that might enjoy it.
River? No. Sam? No. Something just felt
wrong about giving it to them. Then I
remembered Nils's relationship to his
Jaguar spirit. So I offered it to him
the next day.
He looked at it for a while. He saw what
I saw but didn't say too much and ▓

handed it back to me. Thanking me for
the gesture.

I thought back to NuNu and his
father → a plant master... This must
not be a coincidence. This spirit came
from them.

I remembered talking with Sam earlier
about how I/or anyone should be cautious
when picking a shaman to ~~work~~ work with.
Not all have good intensions. There are
a lot of people out there that can cause
bad things to happen to you. Some with
intension, some because they are not experienced
enough to work with the medicine.

I was grateful to trust the shamans here
and I knew they would help me get rid
of this necklace.

It didn't feel like an evil spirit ~~is~~
Just a bad hitchiker or something
mischevious. I was blown away this happened.
And I realized how powerful, mysterious
and dangerous the Amazon ~~is~~ is.

This is the heart of so much ancient wisdom.
It's hard to put the feeling into words. It's
a spirit world here and it's a harsh place to
live. I feel like if the wrong fly landed

on me, I brushed into the wrong plant,
I could pick up a hitch hiking spirit.
Everything here is so alive. And my sensitive
spirit feels ill equipped to safely navigate
this place. I'm a little too in tune. maybe I'm projecting.
I can only imagine the life of a shaman here
The intense sacrifices they have made
and the crazy spirit world they embody
An invisable world of spirits, like
and live with here. ~~the~~ ~~the~~ the tree of
life in Avatar next to a quicksand pit
of pythons. Good or bad, both are so
intense and everywhere. What a crazy
energy this place has. Especially at night.

●●●

Eventually, I made my way to the bathroom
and ~~for the first time~~. Violently puked.
I felt so clean after. I felt like I had shaken
off any bad juju.

After I exited the bathroom, ~~she~~ Ise went
in ~~and~~ and took out the bowl of water
in there. She poured it out and rinsed it
with fresh water. A ritual they do
to capture and get rid of any bad
spirits from my purge.

I decided to spend the night on my
ceremony bed until the spirit was
removed from my Tambo.

When It was my turn to share at the following Sharing circle, I requested that I would only feel comfortable sharing if there was no commentary... and directed this at Chad in front of the group. The last time I shared I did not like the way he spoke to me.

when I finished Chad said "I don't care, I'm going to speak". I responded with a firm "No", "I don't want that". and he proceeded to talk anyhow. I was so <u>angry</u>. I stood up and was about to leave, but decided it would be more powerful to stay. So I paced the room, processed this, and sat down. At one point he crossed the line refering to "you Americans"... "We cause all the problems here".........

Deep Breath.

I had told the group I was content with my journey and it had come to a close and I would leave after the weekend... That is, I said this before Chad

spoke out.

After Chad was done speaking I
spoke back out, ~~and~~ which was ~~not~~
unusual) for the group pattern, and said
"Chad, you are my trigger here."
He then went on to say his thing is
"Tough love"   what a messy Journal
~~page!~~

~~[scribbled out lines]~~

I tried a technique on him. → "You
are all these good things... But, your
crossing the line here..."
It went back and forth → the point is
that I'm proud of my ~~Approach.~~ ~~Even though~~
~~its hard to remember it here exactly.~~

I know he cares. He has shown to
have a caring heart. And I knew
that this was an opportunity to try
standing up for myself and protect
my values. my authentic self. His
response show's me that Taylor will
probably respond poorly to this style.

So now I ponder → Do I stay?
to work on experimenting with
Chad as my trigger? Or leave,
because I don't need someone like Chad
in my life? Do I want to stay for
a new plant Dietas? If so, I shouldn't
let him get in my way.

Normally, I stand up for myself. But
I think that just fueled him.
At one point with him, I practiced hearing
his message when he spoke, his "intensions",
but ignoring his words. This works for
much of his speaking. █ It's a good
general technique.

Carthy agrees but shared his technique
and says people like him don't bother him
because:

If I respect you, you can
trigger me. BUT, if I do
not respect you. You can
not ~~affect~~ me.
     Trigger
Carthy just doesn't let it get to
him. It can still affect you. You just don't
let it trigger you. Let it go.

Magic is real and abundant here.

Rina is leaving here learning to stop taking care of her family in an unhealthy way. To Just "love" them, is all they need. She doesn't want to do "Sales" anymore. She loves children. So she is going to change her work to involve Kids.

The ceremony songs are not from the shamans, but come from Aya herself.

Two more take aways from my ceremony: 1) I don't want to be a shaman. Their dedication to plant medicine is undeniably awe inspiring, but difficult.
2) I think I may be more open to recognizing bad spirits I just got a small lesson.

Ajo Sacha Dietas is over now with lime and salt. 🐸

im Happy. I LET GO.

Carthy = Karthi His advise worked!

I've been passing around Rick Rubins book, the book Ramon said I wasn't ready to read. I can not wait to leave here and read it.

Chad is no longer reactive to me. I was able to put that theory to action overnight. im still figuring out how to understand how its Done exactly. But I Did it!. He even tried to trigger me when I told him this morning I was going to stay, but nothing. it didn't Affect me. I'm Free.

There are magical, unclaggable Toilets here.

+1 647 997 0874

Karthi Karunakaran

I'm powerful enough to manifest my own story The weekend is fun! There are 4 of us 6 more come tomorrow singing, listening to R.Kelly and dancing in the rain

If I can manifest this story, I have the power to manifest my life! Dancing all over the property. Feeling so good. I was reading about how the Incas regard the Coca as the divine plant. Part of every aspect of their life and culture. How chewing Coca is part of their daily lives and how shamans read their leaves. I really want to try it. Maybe I can find some at the Belen Market... famous for selling everything from the amazon.

WOAH

I've worked with weather enough to understand how to request or comunicate w/th it, but this request, like some other forms of manifestation came so quickly... It's amusing how this came up. Sure enough, after dinner, Chad pulled out a big bag of leaves and asked us if we wanted to chew some Coca! ...

I really want to figure out how to bring this powerful me; This manifesting me, back to society. There is just something about nature that works for me.

When I told Karthi how I can unlock closed doors, it occurs to me now that I can and have use my gifts in society as well. Maybe its all about freeing myself from my triggers? Even if not, it will certainly help

Triggers

If you have _power_ over me,
you will trigger me. But,
if you do not have _power_
over me, you will _not_
trigger me.   (-Karthi)

But 1st, you must understand what power
it has over you. Then, you can let it go.
This will work for my money ~~blockage~~ triggers.
I get to use Chad as my test bunny for
this philosophy.

Ajo Sacha (1st Dieta)

Blood purifer. rids body of toxins (spiritual +
physical). Restores strength lost through
blood illnesses. Takes you out of "bad luck".
Enhances hunting skills. It's "a plant of stalking."

I'm not really interested in any more physical pain
from the Aya. There are 3 more ceremonies to
go. It seems a bit unusual to people here. Most
have no physical pain at all, only psychological.
Something just feels off to me. We also learned
they allow women on their period to partake
in ceremony, which is normally a hard **NO** in
Aya Ceremonies. The shamans here feel they
can handle this period power... but maybe it
still affects me? I dunno. Trust feels a little
broken here w/ Chad. But if the shamans
truely knew about her period. I do trust them

I taught Ise how to dive today and she experianced one perfect dive.

~~Am I needy?~~

It's been clear to me for a long time that people don't understand me when they meet me ~~often~~ I see them truely for who they are and it can confront them in strange ways. For Chad, he thinks, at least its been insinuated through Sam, that our group is difficult. Upon looking deeper, I am going to assume that maybe they think I am "entitled" by my approach here the 1st Day with Chad. I triggered him. And so did others. It seems this ? is here to teach Chad but he is not trained to help us or himself. I really have to "assume", maybe, I came off to "needy"! which for me as a paying customer in a vulerable space, I only communicated when I didn't know what to do. Anyhow... it's their issues they need to work on, projected at me. BUT am I needy? Maybe. At times Ida need comfort. This will have to be a question for people I respect. Moana?... Karthi says no I , however think I may be at times.

NO

The time had come for me to decide if I was going to stay or go for the coming week. I decided if I was going to dieta → I would stay.

At the time I was about to drink came my moment of truth. And "Fuck this" I am an adult and don't have to/want to pay to deal with this shit. I'll leave.

When I told Allison she was adamant I drink my dieta as Ramon wanted me on it so he could work on me during ceremony.

It was clear if I stayed there was more work that could be done. So I will stay.

~~This is something I'll address at home. here.~~ And ponder

Chad attacked hard this morning and it was super challenging... Bring it on. I suppose? Annoying really. It took me an hour to shake it. I can do better. I wanted to leave.

The next group is coming today. There will be 1 girl among 8 guys. Knowing Aya, I bet she has issues with men.

NO → I do not agree with my thoughts on the previous page. They were projected onto me and writen in a triggered state.

Edward stood up and ~~said~~ expressed something that his unconsious knows he shouldn't. Something he is working on correcting in himself. In that moment he realized his error. Sat down and a blue butterfly landed on him. Kissing his face. It was beautiful to watch.

Chad teamed up with his workers to repremand Edward for his "issues". What terriable ~~that~~ people. ↳ people

↓

He is trying to establish his dominance before the new group comes. I see his intension. To create a safe space for the ~~■~~ new;

Magical Blue Butterfly
I wear one of my Yagua necklaces every day here.

→ But what about the old?

The sound of frogs playing ping-pong at night.

Chad told Karthi: "you're doing the work." But what Karthi heard is "you're being quiet and obediant".

I really like the energy of this new group.

They removed the bad spirit during the last ceremony.

I know the shamans are working on me when I am unaware.

I decided NOT to drink in the 4th Aya ceremony. It feels nice to get some strength back. And there is other work being done here.

Everything is green/yellow/brown except the blue butterfly. It landing in front of my face during Ramons healing. It's the prettiest creature here.

You can really feel others energies here. And you are aware how powerful touch or someones vibe can transfer it.

The songs of all the birds here. Beautiful.

Book: untethered soul. The power of now.

I have no anxiety here

I'm enjoying thanking my food
I don't think I need Hallusinogens anymore

I feel really Healthy and in tune.

Aya is an intelligent being that we can communicate with. Same with nature.

I don't need to look anymore

my wife is an incredable being

I ~~feel~~ AM my authentic
self.

I feel healthy. Alive. Happy. Free. light.

If I am my authentic self, then I will
harmonize with modern society!!! ██████
   ex: to understand death, one must first
      understand life.

... ████████████████
~~on this~~.

(M) T (W) T (F) S S ⟹ ceremony days

• If I am ▓ my authentic self, than I won't
be triggered by Taylor!!! ~~maybe~~?

• I really enjoy listening, and its what I am
mostly doing here. ████████

• I like Feyyaz. He sees   ~~is that ego?~~
that (I) "you are awake".   ● sitting on the
and said I am the 1st   ● steps listening
person he has ever met   ● to one of the
like this. He is also   workers play
pretty wise. I look forward guitar. ...
to having a conversation   La Casa
with him. It feels good to be seen. Pring ⟹
I sent him an energetic   San Pedro in
vibration from across   Cusco. is where
the pond and he said   ▓ Feyyaz went.
he picked it up without   ⌐The sound of¬
my acknowledgment of it!   crickets at
   CRAZY! Telepathy!   ⌐ night ¬

WOAH

I woke up in the middle of the night to the sound of a powerful force slammed into the floor of my tambo. There are spirits here that travel with the rain...unlike anything I've felt before.

Earlier in the night I relaxed in my hammok and watched the night. I wanted the rain to come, and come down hard. So I requested it... again... for the third time since ive been here. ~~For what purpose?~~ ~~For fun = selfish?~~ ~~Use of natures energy~~

Edward hollered over to me to ask if I was ok. He thought that my Tambo had collapsed. Others heard it too, Karthi was to scared to check it out.

I was scared too. I knew something slapped the wood floor next to my bed so I got up, turned on a light, and looked around. Nothing in my room could have made that noise... It was hard to go back to sleep. It was one Hell of a loud cracking "Boom" sound next to me. Like nothing I've ever experienced.

One of the reasons i've come here is to understand my powers... to find a teacher, to find guidence with them.

I believe I was reprimanded by the spirit ~~of~~ ~~the~~ that traveled with the rain. Maybe I can't request such things without an offering... a sacrifice. maybe I have no idea what the spirit wanted.

For this weeks Dietas with I am not trained. Planta Da Vida, I offered to give up (I can't pork in return for a healthy long know life and I believe that stems from why) getting rid of my Anxiety.

I believe this is a sign too, that if I want to learn more about my abilities, Ayahuasca can teach me... just as she showed me how to see (better) bad → the necklace / the Boon in the rain. spirits... I've been shaking all morning at this thought. ~~~~ I look forward to todays breathwork to bring me comfort.

Watching Feyyaz burn his journal. watching that letting go. Also helped.

Feyyaz said my vibration, my light, is so strong..."How can everyone here, not see it. It permeates the whole space."

There was also a dream last night during the ~~rain~~ thunder storm. The spirit of the rain seduced me until I released. A misgerious spirit. I beleive, but am not sure, this happened after the ~~seed~~ noise.

BREATH WORK

wow.

Moana, you are a gift to
the world.

I AM A TEACHER

I AM POWERFUL

I want to share what I know

I've been pacing back and forth trying to decide if I am going to drink tonight. Do I want to open this door to the spirit world more? Will I if I take ayahuasca? I've been warned by Kevin that once you open that door, you can't close it.

one of the guys <u>Pierce!</u> asked me if I had spoken to Ramon. He only speaks spanish and I've been intimidated by him, so I've been avoiding speaking to them.

This friend speaks spanish so ~~we~~ decided to go find him.

Ramon said he had been waiting to speak with me <u>all day</u>. It was sunset now and almost time for ceremony. He said the spirit that visited me last night was "DIABOLICAL"...

Fuck. I knew it.

He said it didn't matter if I drank tonight or not. Either way I would see visions. The choice is up to me. His advise was, in regards to dealing with them: "use your mind, not your heart."

He said either way, in ceremony I would be opened up in the ceremony...

A couple months ago I met a much more evil spirit at my friend Marins

- Why are these bad spirits coming to me?
- Any advise/wisdom for me to take home?
- Is there any way I could directly reach you if I need to in the future?

I want to revisit my dream in more detail:

A pretty dark hair, dark eyed woman, about 7 years younger then I seduced me. She was a Demon, diabolical spirit in disguise.

Leading into, ~~this~~ and up to, this trip I had obstained from making love to my wife or masterbation. It was advised for Ayacuasca... I think to keep your power inside you and to be careful with the transfer of energies during sex...

The "woman" didn't care about me. It was if her seduction was an annoyance to her.

We Kissed for a long time. Only our lips. She didn't want to have sex and then she said to do it real quick. She didn't take any pleasure in it and before you knew it, I had ejaculated, woken up from this dream, and had to process it all.

Last week Edward went out to pee next to my Tambo and swears a "being" was standing right in front of him. It freaked him out so much he cut off his pee stream and went back to his Tambo. This was, again, at night.

I am telepathic.   He knows ~~thinks~~ it was a bad spirit.

ive been barefoot for nearly two weeks   I am the blue butterfly

I am having a hard day. I opened myself up fully during the sharing circle and Chad ripped into me. He told me I'm not doing the work, the diabolical spirit is my creation and proceeded to insult my character in front of the entire group. Honestly, its totally ripped me apart and makes me question if I really did not accomplish anything here.

I am embarrased

I feel like a failure. A lost cause.
I know this not to be true... I think.
I'm the only one here, he says that is not
"doing the work". Have I not gone deep
enough? Is there some trauma I'm supposed
to be addressing? → that I'm missing?
when I look back at my goals:
  - meet my true self
  - unblock my relationship w/ money
  - learn to harmonize w/ modern society
... have I not worked towards these?
Am I supposed to cry and confess to
an understanding of an uglier self? one
that needs to be cleansed? I know I'm
far from perfect. There is always work to do.
(Chad scolded everyone because I)
(had Pierce, that was not Sam or)
(him, translate Ramon to me. This)
(is ridiculous ⇒ we were just talking.)

He and his wife expressed to me how
terriable of an experience they have
had from me, but did not go into details.
Personally, I think they don't understand
or have the tools to work w/ me and
so, I trigger them. But that makes me

feel full of ego when I hear myself reflect on that. I have _never_, in my life, seen someone have such a strong negative reaction to my character. I'm baffled → I'm open. Did I bring the Demon here? How did it pierce through the energetic saftey bubble I always have around me? Feyyaz says ~~I should~~ the goal should be to see angles,

↓ That struck a cord, I don't want to cause pain.
I clearly have the power to affect them this way, so I must have ~~that~~ power to affect others too? Right or wrong... But I've known my character evokes deep emotions for many people. To me, they are people that still have much to learn. I think they have only just started their own personal growth. But now I'm pointing at silly things. I accept that I can bring this reaction out of ~~people~~. Maybe I can't be my authentic self in public? Or have I let ~~their~~ issues ~~permial~~ permiate my mind. It's good to be aware that my energy can effect others like Chad. For the past 5 days I had completly let go of chad control over me ~~and~~ until now. I was so proud of me.

The 5th ceremony

Chad was pushing for me to drink, which is rediculous, but I was truely on the fence until the moment of truth... when I decided to say yes. For me. I was feeling healthy and ~~wanted to be~~ was curious, so I asked Aya to "Teach" me, with possible spirit knowledge, but really I was open to any lesson.

A heavy rain came down as soon as Chad began to pour Ayahuasca for everyone. I couldn't help but feel that diabolical spirits had traveled with it and I considered sleeping in the Maloka that evening to avoid going back to my Tambo.

I drank another half cup and it was the strongest experiance thus far. The visuals were so intense when I clased my eyes. Neon geometric patterns flying at me. So fast, so intense, I couldn't take it. So I sat up and started smoking Mapachos. With my eyes open I began to see the space around me as a similar, but different dimension. Like the "upside down world" in "Stranger things".

Its an alien dimension. Its no wonder we purge → our bodies are not supposed to live here.

As the ceremony came to a close I became excited to go back to my tambo. I was ready to face/fight my Demons. Literaly and metophorically.

I cleared any emotion and had a clear mind as I walked back to my Tambo. If I could face a diabolical spirit, a I could face anything. Taylor has nothing on this!

Back in my tambo I waited. I was aware it didn't matter if I was ~~asleep~~ asleep or awake. They could come for me in both realms.

But they did not. Maybe ~~it was~~ I had already won as soon as I cleared away my fear. A battle of my mind over my emotions.

I was honestly, hoping for some biblical battle lightning strikes. Like Grandolf from Lord of the Rings:

"You shall not pass."

Woah

I woke up this morning angry. Filled with anger... And I noticed that my emotion permeates out of me... like a bubble around me... it's my energy field. This anger... this emotional field I have, can transmute through the entire center here. I realize now how Feyyaz was "awake" enough to see my field. How he said he could see me vibrate to the entire center and he expressed "How could anyone here, not see you" when he refered to the energetic vibrations I was giving off. And they were happy, warm vibrations...

Now, however, I'm upset and aware Just how much my Feelings/Authentic self can effect those around me, regardless of my intensions to effect them. It doesn't seem fair to them. It's not personal. Moana obviously picks up on it. I don't want my feelings to effect her. And she is more in tune to these emotions than others.

I suppose, when I came here, I was covered in mud, like the River Spirit in the movie "Spirited away". It took the 1st week to clean me and by the second week I felt like myself again.

when I arrived at Mindscape, they had never worked with someone like me. They felt how "heavy" my energy was. They interpreted my energy as "heavy". My energy field is so strong, it was more than Chad was comfortable working with.

I don't believe he has been able to see clearly in my presence since. I get it now. I see why people can have such a difficult time meeting me. And how my ~~emotional state~~ Neurodivergency can shift that experience.

Most people are not "in charge" of healing me. All they need to do is experience me. Chad may be open to experience my field through enough Aya drinking... but...

And in this moment, Feyyaz walked by and I shared this part of my journal with him. It resonated with him. In regards to Chad - "He is mirroring my old energy and you(I) don't like what you(I) have been." ... He suggested asking Aya, "Why do I question myself so much?" Why do I let others affect me and make me question myself?

I see where he is leading, but I am uncertain if I still let people affect me so much anymore. My TRAUMA from childhood is my biggest trauma. I was put in a box by those who didn't understand me, ~~and~~ and ~~often~~ put down so I could stay ~~there.~~

Even if I can not articulate ~~perfectly~~ my question to Aya at tonights ceremony, she is wise enough to see through to my question.

I don't want to bring this energy to breakfast. Its not fair to the rest of the souls who are in their own ~~trauma.~~ Feyyaz is trained enough to understand when an energy is foriegn and to not let it affect him. ~~Not everyone~~ Most people can feel it, but dont understand it. Often, internalizing it as their own.

I'm gonna go dance, shake off this energy, and meditate. There is still work to do.

Today I will just give everyone love. even Chad.

I went to shower and bumped into
Pierce.. I love him! such a gentle warm
soul. I gave love and we spoke. I realize
that chads talk to me woke me up. I got
to see my old energy 1st hand. From a
Healthy space... and it triggered me!
what a gift for him to hold onto
his triggered state for ▇ me to see.
Pierce told me how much he enjoys me
and he sees how powerful I am. My
energy. It brings him comfort when I
drank last night. Knowing we all
went through it together.
              I feel good. I feel like
              my Authentic self again.
I bumped into Josie and gave her love. This
feels good. I love giving love to people. I
explained lightly what happened in the
sharing circle. I think it helped her
understand what happened in there. For her,
it was out of the blue → Chads responce.

After a long meditation I entered a
transient state. First I sent a telopathic
message to Feyyaz "Can you hear me?"
But I knew his antenna was not listening
consciously. It was breakfast and he loves

to interact with everyone. If he was
in a quiet peaceful state... he would have
felt it. So I then sent love to everyone
at breakfast. It was easy to transmit
across the pond from my tambo.

To Chad and Allison: Let go of my
energy. it does not belong to you. I
love you both.

my hemorroids went away... but now, this
morning → a HUGE one. My negative emotions →
are they fueling it? Is it just the Aya?
Feyyaz is the 1st person I have ever met
that speaks more then he listens, yet
that is not the case. To my time experiance,
Yes this is true, but for him, when he
listens, he is actually taking in so much,
He is listening more then he is speaking.
When he does speak, he is always teaching.
The only person I've ever met that
speaks, or appears to speak so much,
but not out of a defense mechanism,
just to share wisdom... and its welcomed.
Tonight - is my last ceremony here, but
also the last for the year at Mind -
scape. The last for Ramon, Lucia, Chad...
It will be a powerful one.

Everyone is telepathic. It happens all the time... I was "just thinking about" you... and "wow, you called".
When I meet people, because I understand the power of my energy field. It will now be "nice to meet you" and a ~~subconscious~~ (see) "I love you". This is the ~~way~~. telepathic

Moana — I'm sorry. you've had to navigate this energy field of me, with me. I understand now. For all the difficult times → I am sorry... and Thank you.
      I am sorry. Thank you.
Chad. I am sorry. Thank you.
  Allison. Sam. Ise. I am sorry. Thank you.
  Chad. I can't believe I'm saying this, but thank you.

          Please forgive me.

I am sorry Moana for bringing you down. For overshadowing your own energy field. For all the trauma I brought to you.

These medicines. These connections to nature are what can really heal.

Karthi and I are Feyyaz's 1st friends he's ever had deep spiritual conversations with. He's 44 (?) years old.

Karthi came to Mindscape to find Elders, He is 35, he got Feyyaz and I.

One guy came to "Feel". He doesn't feel any excitement. 5/10 on his scale. Is where he always exists. The last Aya ceremony got him excited for his trip to the Galapagos.

Casa Del Gasto - Aya retreat where the Canadian Indigenous goes. Seems like a safe place.

Ken Wilber → listen to him. how Feyyez knew he was awake.

Neville Goddard - Manifester

When I "Move", I shake off Energy.

"Purging is a Privilege"

"Icaros" - is the proper name for the songs they sing in ceremony which are taught to them by the plants

speaking to the weather, its telepathy. Thats
how you do it. manifesting is telepathy. when-
ever I think of someone, and I reachout to
them in that moment, they often say
"crazy, I was just thinking about you".

Feyyaz said the next time a foriegn
thought comes into his mind out of
the blue →he's going to try and understand
where it comes from. They can come from
the source, other people, yourself, plants...
your mind is just a filter.

I spoke to Chad and Allison. Apologized
we smiled. Hugged we are all good.

I'm still scared to come home to you
moana. I don't want to trigger you or
get in the way of your healing.

The final Ceremony

The final ceremony came and went pretty
quickly. I was exhausted. Two weeks here
had wiped me out pretty good. My mind was
on Moana. We had spoke during the day and
she was feeling really sick and down. I
really carry her feelings with me. I couldn't
shake them so I embraced them. All the
love I have for her mixed with all the
sadness I carry for my past.
I asked Aya to let me be the puriest
form of my soul. This was my intension

There was light visuals, no pain, and as always, plenty of "purging". By the time it was for individual healing chants from the shamans, I was already asleep. The work and dedication these shamans do is unparalled to any healers I have met. Yesterday they removed a Demon that was hanging on to ~~far~~ this chest. In ceremony they protect the space from bad spirits. Blowing them away, like misquitos buzzing around your head as you walk through nature an hour after twilight. Digesting them and spitting/coughing them out. There is so much strength in their voice. ~~their~~ breath. They are almost not of this world. Their

| Chad + Taylor = Bullies |

Moana, you are the wisest being I know.

Today, I leave. I asked Ramon for a
my apology to healing (with no translator)
Chad was not and he expressed to me
only for myself, that I'm healed. There is
but to clean our nothing for him to work on.
energy for every
one before we The shamans on Aya Flow
did the final are snake charmers.
ceremony together Of course! Pushing back my
Chads methods worked flight was Free. I am
for me. I am manifesting

Thoughts/Reflections:

- What really triggered Chad : (moanas Help)
  → Chad was not used to me. He had never
met a neurodivergent person such as
myself. I showed up authentically me. with
questions, concerns and curiosity. It was a lot
for him to understand someone like me.
If I told him, I was autistic, I would bet
he would have been more open and
understanding. I realize now that my
apology was not nessusary as I did not
do anything wrong, however Chads experience
of me triggered him. Hard. I still took
deep lessons on how my energy can and has
effected moana and I can take away so
much from that — which I've mentioned before.
Plus it helped to alleviate any bad energy
between us so that would not affect
the others in the Ceremony. However, my
experience through all of this was misguided
by Chad and other peoples opinions of
whom or what I am. This is so frustrating
and confusing. This misaligns my entire
experience ... in a way, but does not take
from it overall. So I take back "I am sorry".
and replace it with → Fuck you. you owe me
an apology. This is just like my bullies when I
was young. He is them. I'm reexperianceing my
youth. Woof → what an experiance. He took some of
my experience away and made it his
narritive. He prevented me from being me
which kept me down. I was trapped at
   Mindscape the same way I was trapped in

my elementary school. I used tools I've
learned from an adult to navigate him
but most didn't work. I tried my best
here but my childhood traumas got to me.
what he said to me in that sharing circle
was a fabrication based on his own
insecurities. Fuck that shit.
This might explain some of the reasons I
did not experience any epiphanies with Aya
in some of the ceremonies... I dunno... Maybe
thats a stretch.
Chads approach was always <u>wrong</u>.

• Karthis observation: Aya is a parasite and
we are the host. Lucia agitates Aya and
makes her work inside you while Ramon,
they take turns, heals you, rests you, gives
you knowledge... They go back and forth.
• I feel healthy and when I return home I have
to "do the work" to maintain that. Breathwork. Meditation. Tia Chi. Chi Gong. Healthy
diet. etc. oR, I will lose my mental health.
• Advise from P/F/Karthi: "shed the shield" as
the canadian indigenous said to Pierce, Feyyas,
Karthi and myself at breakfast after telling them
my new thoughts on Chad. They think he showed me
I am still holding trauma from my childhood
bullies. He said to "stop focusing on the spirit
world" and to "work on your shit". To work
on trauma from my past. Chad showed me that
my shield is there. Through time, spirits
have come to protect me/my sheild, but its
time to address this issue. when I can let
this go → I'll be free.

In order to unblock me, I need to get to a state where Chad cannot trigger me. Or at least understanding this may be enough to start letting go. The bullying is the work I need to address. The shield which ~~this~~ has protected my heart and soul. This will be shed!

- my ojai psychic reading: "your coming into your psychic abilities" was a fleeting moment in my reading, but I really held onto the excitment of that. And it is exciting, but...

- Aya, via Mindscape, has shown me the shield, which I never new was there... It makes so much sense. It holds me back. Time to address it.

- I AM IN THE FLOW OF MONEY $ $ $ $ $

- Moana knows me so well, she just wants to protect me. I see her point, agree with it, but my friends were able to show me and say "No". Chad is still right. Work on your bullies.

- However, after a nights sleep - I don't know if my friends are ~~entirely~~ correct. Even Pierce was triggered during Chads attack on me. Isn't it ok to feel hurt/triggered when anyone attacks your character in such a way? Is the path to a pure enlightened self to never get triggered? ~~maybe~~.

- Aya calls you. ~~She works on you regardless if you drink her so long~~ as she only wants to work with those ready to "do the work". For me, it seems little of my work was done drinking Aya. It is not always that case → some really benefit from drinking her. I do think she may have re-programmed me. unconsciously. It was the people, the center, my commitment to heal, the shamans who continued to work on me when I was aware, but also unaware. It was

holding time and space to look within,
sacrificing so much for the betterment
~~[redacted]~~
~~[redacted]~~

of myself. Aya is a
curious medicine
and one I'm uncertain
if I'll drink again. But I wouldn't trade

~~[redacted]~~

my experience for anything in the world.
• The more I reflect → the more I align
with it was wrong of Chad; moanas
insights were on point. My friends are
wise enough, but in the end → I know
me. Moana does too. I am not certain I
need to work on my bullies trauma. I
beleive I am past that. But I do need
to continue to believe in myself, which I
always do... but in this space → I needed
support... and I made some great friends
from it. Chad did help me see my energy in
a different perspective and I'm grateful for
~~[redacted]~~ that.

Aya is a tool. ~~[redacted]~~ To use to get better. But
she is sooo much more.

Aya started her work on me as soon as
I committed to her calling. As soon as I started
my two week diet for her, an offering. A
sacrifice to her. Even now, she is bringing my
parents closer to me, as they try to understand
this journey... they will begin to understand
me better. She is helping Maana heal too. She
has the power to help those around me heal.
without drinking. Just because of me. me
and Aya. Our symbiotic relationship.
She brought those special people together
for a reason. Everything had a purpose. Josie,
needed to work on her relationship with
men. Pierce was only comfortable with women
energy. Cleary this all guys + 1 girl group had
purpose. Every one I met in the street. Every
place I went. It was all aligned.
If I want to continue this relationship with
Aya, with myself, I need to bring this work
back home. Continue to respect the food I
eat, my mental health (meditation), to take
care of my soul and mind. The spirit of
Aya will continue working with me. I have
not given her enough credit. She is so much
more then an experience through a drinking
ceremony. She is a spirit. She works in
many ways.

I need to stop doubting myself and respect my
intuition more. To work on my vocabulary and
belief system. Nothing negative.
Manifest every part of my life.

Anyone that does Aya. Its all about intension. Your offering to her, your sacrifices are important.

I'm so powerful right now. So connected. I'm bringing this home. I can't wait to go home!

I feel amazing. So light. So Bright. Vibrating with a light energy that permiates every cell in my body. Smiling. Happy. Alive. In tune.

Drinking Aya: There are 3 main things happening during ceremony: Trauma, Shamans working on us, Reprograming. But it its important to understand that drinking Aya is new to non-shamans. Its new to people like me. I'm not even sure the shamans think we need to drink it. The shamans only begin to drink Aya after many years of Dieting (Dietas) on many plants. They often start young. Lucia started when she was 9. After years of learning to connect with many plant spirits, then they begin to drink the Master of all plants: Ayahuasca. Traditionally, they drink Aya to understand how to treat a patient of theirs. This has always been the way until recently.

When an untrained drinker, such as myself, drinks Aya... It reprograms your brain. I can't explain how. But it does. It also shocks our system and that causes trauma. Which we internalize and relate to in our own way. Forcing our mind to experiance old trauma... and we think on it... and try to address it. When you get comfortuble and advanced

Continued from
my Journal...

enough — you can begin to speak with Aya and form an alliance with her. Asking for direct help from her and other plant medicines.

And then, there are the shamans. They are sooo essential. They must be the most trusted you can find. They take the Aya inside you and work on you with it. Without them, you may just experiance trauma. But with them, they will cut into your soul with a scalpel. They will remove what does not belong. Reprogram what needs adjustments. Your trust in them is essential.

At Mindscape there are
two shamans for 8-10
people during a six hour
ceremony. I can't imagine
a singular shaman in a
20-40+ person ceremony.

I am grateful for all the
attention such a small group
allowed healing for. With
an unexperienced Shaman,
I worry that a portal is
open and they may not
be able to safely protect
the people drinking it.

And then, there is the 4$\underline{\underline{th}}$
thing. What happens before
and after the ceremony.
The mystical, unexplainable
but seemingly obvious
work she does. The
work I've recently

explained. The work that
is hard to explain to
a non-believer.

〰〰〰〰〰〰〰〰〰

$$ I am in the flow with $$
MONEY

〰〰〰〰〰〰〰〰〰

I'm not coming back to
the Amazon without
spiritual protection. A
form of energy shield.
How do I do that? ⤵

No Idea

———————//———————

There was an <u>orange cat</u>
begging for food the past
two nights since I've
been back in Iquitos. I
decided I'd feed him tonight.
Orange cats are special,
but something seemed

off. Malnourished →
sure, but it was in the
eyes. Eyes of fire. I've
never seen a cat like
this... and then I
realized → TRUST
         YOURSELF.

<u><u>Listen to your instincts.</u></u>

This cat feels wrong.
Bad. Devil like.

And I remembered a few
weeks back seeing some
local women, Elders,
sitting peacefully sewing
Icaros on the street,
but when this cat came
around... they scared it off
with aggression. I had
never seen anything like

it. ~~Almost like~~ they
knew it was evil.

And then, I knew.
NO.
I don't want to have
anything to do with
this cat.
I told it to scram! and
one of the elder ladies,
again, helped shoo it
away too. She knew.
I knew.

| Trust my instincts. |

my intuition

Bad can hide itself
any where, but I can see
it now.

———————— // ————————

Over the past few days,
after leaving Mindscape,
I've been spending time
with friends reflecting
in Iquitos.

I had just recieved a
custom lamp order and
it was a special one so
I explained my   ↓
buisness to   (a pendant)
them. I had
recently learned that
artists should always
have a 'Hail Mary' peice.
Something big/bold/
expensive, that when
purchased would allow
the artist to continue
growing.

That peice is my Floor
Lamp and I've never sold
one.

~~And then the following day~~

Feyyaz has the craziest sugar addiction. I've never seen anything like it. We would frequently stop by this one Ice cream shop to feed his addiction (his Joy?).

... Anyhow, this afternoon, the day after I explained my buisness to my friends. I got another order.

A FLOOR LAMP!

my clients name was Ari... and as Karthi and I headed to dinner, sharing the exciting news, we passed the Ice cream parlor one last time. It's name: Ari's

———————— // ————————

I've been sleeping, well
half asleep, for a few
hours on this plane ride
home. I have an aisle seat
and out of the blue, a
~~thought~~ comes to my mind:

   what if the woman
   next to me has to
   go to the bathroom?

Imeadiatly, after this
thought arose I got a tap
on my shoulder,

            and I know...

A portrait of myself (author) in front of my
tambo by Feyyaz. 2023.

www.ingramcontent.com/pod-product-compliance
Lightning Source LLC
Chambersburg PA
CBHW061735120626
46550CB00005B/1805